D0383042

NO LONGER PROPERTY
OF ANYTHINK
RANGEVIEW LIBRARY
DISTRICT

MILITARY ENGINEERING
☆ ☆ ☆
IN ACTION

MILITARY SUBMARINES

SEA POWER

Taylor Baldwin Kiland and Michael Teitelbaum

Enslow Publishing
101 W. 23rd Street
Suite 240
New York, NY 10011
USA
enslow.com

Published in 2016 by Enslow Publishing, LLC.
101 W. 23rd Street, Suite 240, New York, NY 10011

Copyright © 2016 by Enslow Publishing, LLC.

All rights reserved.

No part of this book may be reproduced by any means without the written permission of the publisher.

Library of Congress Cataloging-in-Publication Data

Kiland, Taylor Baldwin, 1966-
 Military submarines : sea power / Taylor Baldwin Kiland and Michael Teitelbaum.
   pages cm. — (Military engineering in action)
 Includes bibliographical references and index.
 Summary: "Describes the development, use, and abilities of submarines in the military"—Provided by publisher.
 Audience: Grades 7-8.
 ISBN 978-0-7660-6918-3 (library binding)
 ISBN 978-0-7660-7069-1 (pbk.)
 ISBN 978-0-7660-7070-7 (6-pack)
 1. Submarines (Ships)—United States—Juvenile literature. 2. United States. Navy—Submarine forces—Juvenile literature.
 I. Teitelbaum, Michael. II. Title.
 V858.K55 2015
 359.9'3830973—dc23
                         2015011222

Printed in the United States of America

To Our Readers: We have done our best to make sure all Web site addresses in this book were active and appropriate when we went to press. However, the author and the publisher have no control over and assume no liability for the material available on those Web sites or on any Web sites they may link to. Any comments or suggestions can be sent by e-mail to customerservice@enslow.com.

Portions of this book originally appeared in *Submarines: Underwater Stealth*.

Photo Credits: AFP/Stringer/Getty Images, p. 45; CHOI JAE-HO/AFP/Getty Images, p. 6; Class Tristin Bomar/US Navy via Getty Images, p. 22; Courtesy of USNHC and chinfo.navy.mil, p. 15; De Agostini Picture Library/De Agostini/Getty Images, p. 47; Designua/Shutterstock.com, p. 20; MIL Pictures by Tom Webber/The Image Bank/Getty Images, p. 7; National Archives and Records Administration/Wikimedia Commons/Holland (SSI). Starboard bow, on ways, 1900 - NARA - 512954.tif/Public Domain, p. 14; Science & Society Library/ SSPL/Getty Images, p. 12; Shutterstock.com (art/backgrounds throughout book): Dianka Pyzhova, Ensuper, foxie, kasha_malasha, pashabo; US Navy photo, pp. 19, 30; US Navy photo by Chief Mass Communication Specialist Ahron Arendes, pp. 16, 43; US Navy photo by Chief Photographer's Mate Andrew McKaskle, pp. 1 (diver, front right), 4, 8; US Navy photo by Chief Photographer's Mate John E. Gay, p. 38; US Navy photo by Jeremy Lambert, p. 39; US Navy photo by Journalist 1st Class Davis J. Anderson, p. 23; US Navy photo by Mass Communication Specialist 2nd Class Alexia M. Riveracorrea, p. 28; US Navy photo by Mass Communication Specialist 1st Class Jayme Pastoric, p. 26; US Navy photo by Mass Communication Specialist 1st Class John Fields, p. 34; US Navy photo by Mass Communication Specialist 1st Class Joseph M. Buliavac, p. 44; US Navy photo by Mass Communication Specialist 2nd Class Jumar T. Balacy, p. 36; US Navy photo by Mass Communication Specialist 1st Class Mike Lenart, p. 29; US Navy photo by Mass Communication Specialist 1st Class Pete D. Blair, p. 32; US Navy photo by Mass Communication Specialist 2nd Class Ronald Gutridge, pp. 9, 17; US Navy photo by Mass Communication Specialist 1st Class Todd A Schaffer, p. 18; US Navy photo by Senior Chief Mass Communication Specialist Andrew McKaskle, pp. 4,8; US Navy photo courtesy of General Dynamics Electric Boat, p. 1 (submerged submarine, front left); xavier gallego morell/Shutterstock.com, p. 2 (submarine).

Cover Photos: US Navy photo by Chief Photographer's Mate Andrew McKaskle (front right); US Navy photo courtesy of General Dynamics Electric Boat (front left); Shutterstock.com: kasha_malasha (camouflage background), foxie (series logo), xavier gallego morell (submarine, back).

CONTENTS

A member of SEAL Delivery Vehicle Team Two (SDVT-2) prepares to launch one of the team's SEAL Delivery Vehicles (SDV) from the back of the submarine USS *Philadelphia* on a training exercise.

SEALs and Submarines

The small team of Navy SEALs put on wet suits and scuba gear and attached knives and rifles to their swimwear. They were embarked on the submarine USS *Ohio* somewhere in the Pacific Ocean. Quietly and anonymously, they exited the fleet ballistic missile submarine through an airtight compartment—a converted missile tube—that was then opened to the ocean. Seawater flooded in. This allowed the SEALs to swim out of the submarine without flooding it. They then crawled inside a very small tube attached to the top of the submarine. Called a Seal Delivery Vehicle (SDV), this tube is shaped like a torpedo and can tightly fit up to six SEALs. One of the SEALs navigates this tiny submersible with the help of one rear propeller. The SDV is a "free-flooding" vessel. This means it is filled with water, so the SEALs must use their scuba tanks to breathe. Since a submarine cannot operate in waters shallower than 50 feet (15.24 meters), the SDV allows SEALs to get almost all the way to the beach under the water.

SDVs have been in use for decades. In World War II, the British trained with these types of vehicles, but they never became operational. In Vietnam, they were used for reconnaissance, or intelligence gathering. Today, they are equipped with navigation equipment, sonar, and a docking system that remotely reunites the SDV with the submarine after the SEALs have disembarked from the vehicle.

While the *Ohio* was originally built to host and launch nuclear missiles against the United States' Cold War enemies, the submarine has now been reconfigured as a special operations platform. Both submarines and SEALs have a history in stealth operations—now they are partners!

The USS *Ohio* (SSGN 726) docks at a harbor in Busan, South Korea.

Navy SEALs and Submarines: Partners in Stealth

The Navy SEALs have been operating since 1962. "SEAL" stands for SEa, Air, and Land. These small teams of special forces are usually the first ones to go into dangerous situations. They clear the way for other troops. The SEALs undergo what many consider to be the toughest military training in the world.

In addition to mission training and practice working as a team, each SEAL must endure grueling fitness training. A typical SEAL workout includes swimming 500 yards (457.2 m) in eight minutes, doing one hundred push-ups in two minutes, and running a mile and a half (2.4 kilometers) in under ten minutes. Like the submarines that sometimes carry them to their dangerous destinations, SEALs are powerful and impressive, operating in stealth and secrecy.

This special operation forces combat diver carries a diver propulsion vehicle (DPV) and an automatic rifle.

MK 8 Mod 1 SEAL Delivery Vehicle (SDV)

CAPABILITIES: Can be launched from a dry deck shelter on the back of a submarine, deliver several fully equipped SEALs to the mission area, remain "parked" in the area, and then retrieve the SEALs and return home. SDVs can also be launched from specially equipped amphibious surface ship carriers or airdropped (unmanned) from a cargo aircraft.

POWER SOURCE: Battery

CREW: Up to six crew members

A SEAL Delivery Vehicle team member gets ready to launch a SDV from the USS *Philadelphia*, a Los Angeles-class attack submarine, during a training exercise. The SDV carries Navy SEALs from the submarine to enemy targets.

The Submarine's Role in the War on Terrorism

While the war on terrorism has been largely fought on land, submarines have also played a role. In response to the terrorist attacks on the United States on September 11, 2001, the submarine USS *Key West* was the first ship to arrive off the coast of Pakistan in support of Operation Enduring Freedom. This fast attack submarine launched multiple Tomahawk cruise missiles into Afghanistan. The fast attack submarine USS *Cheyenne* was the first warship to launch Tomahawks into Baghdad, when Operation Iraqi Freedom commenced.

The USS *Cheyenne*

What Is Sonar?

The sonar equipment on a submarine acts as the vessel's eyes and ears when the sub is deep in the dark ocean. It is used to detect the presence and location of objects (usually other subs or ships) under the sea. "Sonar" stands for SOund NAvigation and Ranging.

There are two types of sonar: active and passive. With active sonar, a sub sends a sound pulse out into the water and crewmen listen to see how long it takes for the pulse to bounce off another object and return to the sub. This tells the crew how far away and in what direction the other sub or ship is. If a sub uses active sonar, the sonar on any other sub or ship in the area will detect it and know the sub is out there.

Since the main goal of a sub is to stay hidden and operate in secret, most subs rarely use active sonar. Instead, they use passive sonar. This consists of listening for sounds made by other ships and subs. A skilled sonar operator can figure out another ship's speed and even what kind of ship it is just by listening to the passive sonar.

A Ship That Sinks?

Submarines are like fish; they dive and thrive under the sea. But they are also complex and technologically advanced warships. How do they work? What makes a ship successfully sink, maneuver under the water, and then resurface?

The first military submarine was the *Turtle*, built in 1775. It was also the first American sub. The *Turtle* was about 7.5 feet long, 6 feet tall, and 3 feet wide (2.2 m x 1.8 m x .91 m). Shaped like a giant clam, it was made from two wooden shells covered with tar.

It submerged by allowing water into its hull, or body. Two hand-cranked propellers moved the sub up and down and side to side. To surface, the operator had to pump the water out by hand. This made the *Turtle* lighter so it would rise.

The *Turtle* submersible was a one-man vessel powered by two hand-operated propellers. Foot pumps let in or let out water to control depth. Its purpose was to dive beneath the enemy ship and bore a hole in the hull, in which a 150-pound (68 kg) explosive charge and clockwork timer would be placed.

In 1776, during the American Revolution, David Bushnell, the *Turtle*'s inventor, attempted to use it to sink a British warship in New York Harbor. While underwater, he tried to attach a gunpowder-filled torpedo to the underside of the ship. But the torpedo did not attach properly, so no damage was caused to the British vessel.

During the American Civil War, in the 1860s, the Union army used a twenty-man sub called the *Alligator*. The 47-foot-long (14.3 m) sub was originally powered by oars but was later given hand-operated propellers. The operator in the sub turned a crank, which then turned the outside propellers to power the ship.

The *Alligator* was the first sub to include an airlock from which a diver could exit a sub while underwater to attach mines, or small explosive devices, to enemy ships. An airlock is a small room that can be filled with air or water. When a diver is going to leave a sub, the room is filled with water. Then the door is opened and the diver goes out into the sea. When the diver returns, he enters the airlock, which is again filled with water. The outer hatch is then closed, and the water is pumped out of the airlock. Then the crew opens the inside door, and the diver steps back into the sub. Without an airlock the sub would flood each time a diver went in or out.

The Confederate navy also had a submarine, the USS *Hunley*. In 1864, it was the first combat submarine to sink a warship, the sloop USS *Housatonic*, in Charleston Harbor. However, the *Hunley* sank soon after, killing all eight men aboard, and the ship was lost.

What Powers a Submarine?

A "modern" submarine was invented in the late 1890s. In 1900, the US Navy bought the sub, calling it the USS *Holland* after its inventor, John Phillip Holland. The *Holland* was the first submarine to use a gasoline-powered engine while on the surface and electric battery power for traveling underwater.

In 1904, the French submarine *Aigrette* replaced the gasoline-powered engine with a diesel-powered engine for surface travel. This remained the standard submarine power system for the next

The USS *Holland* goes under construction in 1900.

fifty years. In 1949, Navy Admiral Hyman G. Rickover oversaw the development of nuclear power for submarines. Rickover was called the "Father of the Nuclear Navy." His work led to the creation of the world's first nuclear-powered submarine, the USS *Nautilus*, in 1955.

Before the use of nuclear power on submarines, subs were forced to surface regularly. They needed to fill up with diesel fuel and recharge their electric batteries. Subs also needed to surface frequently to resupply themselves with oxygen so the crewmen could breathe.

Around the same time that nuclear power was added to subs, oxygen generators, which can take oxygen right from seawater, were also created. These two changes allowed submarines to remain underwater for months at a time. They no longer needed to surface to refuel and get fresh air.

The Search for the USS Hunley

After it went down in Charleston Harbor, the USS *Hunley*'s wreckage remained a mystery until 1970 or 1995—depending on whom you believe. Underwater archeologist E. Lee Spence claimed he found it in 1970 and published a map with the location identified. Diver Ralph Wilbanks and novelist Clive Cussler found the wreckage in 1995. A large team of underwater archaeologists and anthropologists began excavation efforts in 2000. They slipped a harness underneath the sunken remains of the sub and raised it with a crane. The submarine resurfaced after more than 136 years underwater. The vessel is now on public display in Charleston, South Carolina.

The Confederate submarine *H.L. Hunley* used a torpedo launched by a pole to sink the USS *Housatonic*.

Most improvements in submarine design since the 1950s have been to the type and number of weapons they are capable of carrying. Since the 1990s, new submarine designs have also reflected changing computer technology.

How Do Submarines Dive?

All submarines contain large tanks called ballast tanks. When the ballast tanks are filled with air, the submarine floats on the ocean's surface, like a regular ship. In order to submerge, a submarine fills its ballast tanks with water. The extra weight from the water causes the sub to sink. When it is time to come back up, the sub blows thousands of gallons of water out of its tanks and rises to the surface.

Submarines are steered from the control room. The helmsman adjusts the rudder, a flap that steers the sub left or right. The planesman adjusts the diving planes, flaps that steer the sub up or down.

Seawolf was the fastest, quietest, most heavily armed nuclear-powered attack submarine in existence when it was commissioned in 1997.

Crew members aboard the attack submarine USS *Santa Fe* look through periscopes for contacts.

When a sub is near the surface it can raise its periscope, a type of binoculars that allow crewmen to see if there are ships or land nearby. When a sub is underwater, sonar helps the sub's crew make its way through the darkness beneath the sea.

Who Works on a Submarine?

A modern submarine like the USS *Cheyenne* carries a crew of 134 people. The crew is made up of 13 officers, who are in command, and 121 enlisted men, who perform the day-to-day work that keeps the sub running.

The crew is divided into different groups based on their jobs. The executive department is in charge of making sure everyone

A logistics specialist conducts an inventory of repair parts and supplies aboard the USS *Helena*.

else does his or her job so that missions go smoothly. The sub's commanding officer, or captain, is in charge of everything that happens on the sub. Every department reports to the captain.

The engineering department makes sure that the sub's nuclear reactor operates safely. Taking care of the ship's torpedoes, missiles, and sonar equipment is the job of the weapons department. The torpedoman's mate, missile technician, and fire control technician all work in the weapons department.

The sub's position is monitored at all times by the operations department. They are also responsible for the communications equipment.

The ship's food and spare parts are managed by the supply department. They cook all the meals for the crew and also take care of the crew's laundry.

Taking care of the crew's health is the job of the medical department. They give the crew regular checkups and treat them when they are sick. They also inspect the sub every day to make sure it is clean and check the quality of drinking water, food, and air so the crew stays healthy.

How Do Submarines Protect Themselves?

Modern subs have four different types of weapons: MK-48 torpedoes, Harpoon missiles, Tomahawk (cruise) missiles, and submarine-launched mobile mines (SLMMs). An MK-48 torpedo operates underwater. It can be used against ships or other submarines.

Off the coast of the Bahamas, the USS *Florida* launches a Tomahawk cruise missile during an experiment to test the capabilities of the US Navy's future guided-missile submarines.

FACT

Nuclear Reactor

Hot coolant

Control rod
(Neutron catchers)

Nuclear fuel

Cold coolant

Moderator

Radiation
protection barrier

How Nuclear Power Works

All nuclear-powered submarines have a nuclear reactor, which generates the electricity that runs the sub. In the reactor, nuclear power is created when the atoms of a metal called Uranium-235 split apart. The splitting of the atoms creates heat. This heat is used to boil water, which creates steam. The steam provides power to turn a turbine, which then turns an electrical generator. The generator makes enough electricity to operate the sub. Uranium-235 is a very dangerous material, but if the nuclear reactor is properly maintained and operated it can be used as a safe source of power.

A Harpoon missile is designed to skim the ocean's surface, then strike and sink warships. Once it is fired, a Harpoon missile's radar automatically turns on to help the missile find its target. The Tomahawk (cruise) missile flies through the air toward a target on land, such as a building.

A submarine-launched mobile mine (SLMM) is used like a torpedo, but only in shallow water. It is used to target opposing submarines.

What Is It Like to Live on a Submarine?

Today, the amount of time a submarine can stay underwater is limited only by the food supply and how long the crew can do their jobs well without a break back on land. That is usually about two months.

On a submarine, a day is eighteen hours long, not twenty-four hours long. Since the sub's crew does not see daylight or night-time, they very quickly get used to this schedule. The eighteen-hour day is divided into three six-hour work shifts called watches. Each crewman is on duty for six hours doing his job. Then he is off duty for twelve hours.

During his off time a crewman will sleep, eat, shower, exercise, attend training sessions, study for promotions, watch movies, or play cards. Subs keep about four hundred movies on board. They also carry board games, video games, and books.

Crewmen also spend a lot of their off-duty time cleaning the sub. Imagine more than one hundred people living together in a small space for two months. Things can get pretty dirty if they are not taken care of. The floors, or decks, are scrubbed, and equipment and living areas are cleaned each day.

Crewmen eat breakfast, lunch, and dinner every day. Crew members going on or coming off watch also eat midnight rations (nicknamed "midrats"). Eggs, pancakes, and cereal are served for breakfast. Deli sandwiches, hamburgers, and pizza are made for lunch. Pasta, steak, chicken, and pork dishes are cooked for dinner. Leftovers are eaten for midrats. Treats like ice cream and soda are also always available.

Crewmen sleep in a section of the sub called the berthing area. Each crewman gets about 15 square feet (1.4 sq m) of space in which to sleep and store his personal belongings. Each crewman's bed (also called a bunk, berth, or rack) has a small reading light. Personal belongings are stored in a locker under the bunk.

Sailors aboard the USS *Ohio* enjoy Super Bowl XLV. The crew eat all meals together every day. Crew members going on or coming off watch also eat midnight rations, or "midrats."

Some bunks are so small that there is not enough room for a crewman to turn over without getting out of bed and getting back in!

A submarine operates around the clock, so about one-third of the crew is always sleeping while the others work. Because of this, lights in the berthing area are kept dim.

On land, submarine crewmen wear the regular white uniforms worn by all sailors in the US Navy. While on the sub, they wear one-piece blue coveralls. Well trained for the operation of the complex machinery of a modern submarine, and working and living together for many months at a time, the crew of a submarine forms a special bond.

Fast Attack vs. Ballistic Missile Submarines

The US Navy has two types of nuclear submarines: fast attack and ballistic missile. Fast attack submarines, also called a hunter-killer submarines, are specifically designed to attack and sink vessels—other submarines and surface ships. At the same time, they can protect other vessels. They are designated with an "SSN" after their names. Ballistic missile submarines are equipped to launch missiles with nuclear warheads. They are designated with an "SSBN" after their names. They are part of the nuclear "triad," the US nuclear arsenal that includes strategic bombers (aircraft), intercontinental ballistic missiles (ICBMs), and the SSBNs.

A SEAL Delivery Vehicle team works on the surface after conducting training drills with sailors on the USS *Toledo* (SSN 769).

Tapping the Soviets: The Story of the USS *Halibut*

I t was 3:00 A.M. one night in 1970, and Navy Captain James Bradley couldn't sleep. He was alone in his office in Washington, DC, but he had an idea that he thought just might change the course of history and help the United States win the Cold War. He wanted to send the submarine USS *Halibut* on a secret and risky mission to search the ocean floor deep inside Soviet-controlled territory for a target that was no more than 5 inches (12.7 centimeters) wide. The *Halibut* was uniquely qualified for this mission, as it was the first sub designed to carry guided missiles, which use built-in radar to find their targets.

The *Halibut* would be sent to the Sea of Okhotsk off the eastern coast of the Soviet Union to search for a telephone cable that ran from a Soviet missile submarine base all the way to Moscow, the Soviet capital, about 3,700 miles (5,955 km) away. (That is about the same distance from New York City to Paris, France!) Captain Bradley knew that if it could tap into the cable, the United States would be able to listen to top-secret Soviet military information.

Secrecy and silence would be the keys to the success of this plan. And nothing was more suited for this type of work than a submarine. In fact, this mission was so secretive that of the 111 men on board, only the sub's commander, Jack McNish, his 14 officers, and the handful of deep-sea divers on the special projects team knew the purpose of the *Halibut*'s operation. The others were told that the divers were there to search for pieces of Soviet missiles.

The divers on board the *Halibut* would leave the sub when it was on the sea floor. There, they would battle the incredible pressure and strong currents near the sea's bottom and attempt to attach a recording device onto the Soviet communications cable.

The sub carried special equipment just for this difficult operation. Because the mission was top secret, this equipment was also kept secret. One such item was the deep-sea divers' decompression chamber. This would allow the divers to prepare for and recover from their underwater mission.

The other piece of special equipment was nicknamed the "fish." This was a device containing a video camera, a photo camera, and lights, which were all attached to a cable. The fish was sent out of the sub so it could search the sea bottom for the Soviet communications cable. Once it found the cable, it would send videos and photos back to the sub.

Arriving in the Sea of Okhotsk, the *Halibut* stayed close enough to the surface to use its periscope. As the sub glided along the Soviet shoreline, Commander McNish peered through the periscope, searching for something on the shore. He knew that the Soviets' underwater cable would be marked with a sign so that ships passing near the shore would not accidentally tear the cable.

McNish found the sign and gave the order for the *Halibut* to submerge. He then ordered the special projects team to launch the

Navy divers walk along the ocean floor during operations.

fish. The small cluster of cameras and lights motored slowly through the dark water, attached to its long cable. For several days, the fish sent back grainy photos and video images of giant crabs and tiny jellyfish.

Only the handful of men who were part of the special projects team were allowed to view these images. The men watched closely, searching for any signs of the Soviet communications cable. About a week after they started searching, the fish sent back images of a bump in the seafloor. Along the bump, like the black dashes of a dotted line, the cable stuck out of the sandy bottom. The *Halibut* had found the cable at last!

The *Halibut*'s crew now had to find a flat stretch of sea bottom near the cable. They stopped the sub above a long flat area, then slowly lowered its two large mushroom-shaped anchors to the seafloor. These would keep the *Halibut* from drifting.

The divers had been waiting in the secret decompression chamber for many hours. Their bodies had to slowly get used to the increased water pressure they would face on the sea's floor.

When they were ready, the divers slipped into rubber suits. Tubes ran through the suits. One tube brought oxygen to the divers' helmets. Another carried communications lines so they could stay in contact with Commander McNish on the sub. One set of tubes contained hot water, which kept the divers warm in the cold seawater.

The suits also contained an emergency line, which could be used to pull the divers back into the sub if something went wrong with their mission. The divers also carried small bottles of emergency air, nicknamed "come-home bottles." These would allow them to breathe for about four minutes if their main oxygen supply failed, enough time to make it back to the sub in an emergency.

Commander McNish gave the order, and the divers slipped from the decompression chamber and out into the sea. They worked for many hours, attaching a recording device to the cable.

Back in the *Halibut*, the helmsman and planesman took readings of the water currents every fifteen minutes. They struggled to keep the *Halibut* steady as the sub swayed against its anchors, pulled by the powerful deep-sea currents.

Finally the divers successfully completed their task. Top-secret Soviet phone calls were now being "tapped," or recorded by the United States. The divers returned safely to the *Halibut*. They spent a few hours in the decompression chamber to get their bodies back to normal. Then the USS *Halibut* headed for home, its mission successfully completed.

When a call for help is received, the US Navy's Deep Submergence Unit, known as the submarine rescue diving and recompression system (SRDRS), can be quickly sent to any location in the world by air or ground and can also go on military or commercial vessels.

The *Halibut* was decommissioned in 1976 and "mothballed," or put in storage. Then, in 1994, this important "weapon" in the Cold War was scrapped. The *Halibut* was taken apart, and its metal was recycled. This is common with older military equipment and does not lessen the valuable service they performed while they were in active use.

Decompression

The water pressure under the sea is much greater than the air pressure on land because of the weight of the water above. When deep-sea divers leave a submarine to explore the ocean's bottom, their bodies must already be used to the increased pressure. A decompression chamber is used to slowly increase the pressure for divers before they leave the sub.

Then, the process is reversed when the divers return. The pressure is slowly lowered in the chamber, and the divers are given oxygen to breathe before they step back into the normal air pressure aboard the sub. If pressure changes too quickly, divers can experience what is known as "the bends." The body releases gas bubbles into the bloodstream that cause difficulty in breathing and can even lead to death.

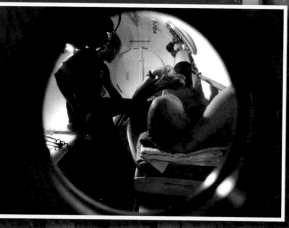

Navy divers conduct decompression sickness training in a recompression chamber.

The USS Halibut (SSN-587)

COMPLETED: 1960
SIZE: Length: 360 feet (109.7 m); Width: 29 feet, 6 inches
(9 m);
Height: 20 feet, 9 inches (6.3 m)
POWER SOURCE: One Westinghouse S3W nuclear reactor
MAXIMUM OPERATING DEPTH: About 700 feet (213.4 m)
MAXIMUM TIME UNDERWATER: 90 days
MAXIMUM SPEED: 15.5 knots (17.9 miles per hour/28.8 kph)
NUMBER OF TORPEDOES/MISSILES: 11

The USS *Halibut* is the first submarine specifically built to serve as a platform for firing guided missiles.

Submarines to the Rescue

I t is the turtle of the submarine community, moving at a walker's pace. It is only 16 feet (4.8 m) long, bright yellow, and the slowest submarine the US Navy has. This sub, however, can dive to depths that no regular submarine can—as deep as 15,000 feet (4,572 m). The Bluefin-21 has no crew and is operated remotely. It can be loaded onto almost any ship and can carry multiple sensors. So, it is not surprising that it was deployed to search for Malaysian Airlines Flight 370 when it disappeared over the Indian Ocean on March 8, 2014, with 239 passengers and crew members on board.

Unmanned aerial vehicles, called drones, have been widely used in the sky to spy on and eliminate opposing forces in the wars in Iraq and Afghanistan, but they have only recently been used under the sea. An unmanned underwater vehicle (UUV) like the Bluefin-21 was the only vehicle capable of scouring the deep, pitch-black ocean floor of the southern Indian Ocean, so it was put to work.

Operators aboard the Australian navy vessel ADF *Ocean Shield* prepare to deploy the US Navy's Bluefin-21.

It took twenty-four hours for the Bluefin-21 to complete each mission. Within two hours it dove 15,000 feet to the bottom of the ocean—farther than any manned submarine can reach. In another sixteen hours, it searched the ocean floor for debris. It took two hours to return to the surface of the ocean, and then it took another four hours to download all the information from the Bluefin-21 to a computer. Not bad for a day's work.

Regular submarines have also been used to find wreckage on the seafloor. As recounted in a 2014 story in *Historic Wings* magazine, an F-14 Tomcat fighter jet slid off the deck of the USS *John F. Kennedy* near the coast of Scotland in 1976. It sank to the bottom of the ocean (the crew ejected safely), along with its revolutionary combat system, including the AIM-54 Phoenix air-to-air missile. At this time in history, the United States was deeply engaged in the Cold War with the Soviet Union. The US Navy was concerned that the Soviets could recover the aircraft and the missile and copy the missile's technology. This could have been a major setback to the US Navy. So, the race was on to salvage the plane and the missile before the Soviets could.

The missing aircraft and its Phoenix missile had sunk in waters as deep as 1,850 feet (564 m). A group of P-3 Orions, antisubmarine aircraft, was deployed to circle the area like hawks. A salvage ship and tugboats were quickly sent to the area, too. They were equipped with sonar to find the aircraft and big nets to scoop it out of the ocean. But the sonar yielded nothing. The plane had disappeared from the location where it sank. What had happened? Had the currents dragged the plane to a new location? Had the Soviets grabbed the plane first?

As the salvage team was scratching their heads, an engineer stationed at Submarine Squadron Two in Holy Loch, Scotland, had an idea: why not use the navy's top secret submarine, the NR-1, to find the plane? The response he received was surprising. Apparently, the NR-1 was so secret that not many people in the navy knew of its unique capabilities, which were perfect for this mission.

Soon, the NR-1 was on its way and began scouring the ocean floor, searching in a box pattern for the plane. The ocean floor was littered with large boulders, however, which made it harder—and more dangerous—to find the missing plane in all the crevices. The whole time, the Soviets were circling the search area, watching the operation closely and looking for any opportunity to sneak in and steal the plane. Within days, the plane was spotted and a trawler was engaged to wrap the plane in a net and drag it to more shallow waters, where it could then be lifted onto a ship. But, there was one problem: the missile was missing!

Nuclear research submarine NR-1 prepares to survey Flower Garden Banks in the Gulf of Mexico.

Once again, the NR-1 started its slow and painstaking search process until it found the missile a short distance away. The submarine proceeded to extend its "keel claw" to clutch the missile and lift it to the surface. This was an extremely dangerous task, as no one knew if the warhead on the missile was armed. If so, it might explode during the recovery effort. The submarine's claw wrapped itself around the missile, clamped gently, and slowly rose to the surface. The mission was timed to finish at midnight so that the Soviets could not get a good photographic image of the top-secret submarine.

Bobbing in the ocean, cables from a salvage ship were attached to the missile and the NR-1's keel claw slowly released it. The missile was gently hoisted aboard the nearby surface ship. The F-14 was also safely recovered. No vessel other than the submarine NR-1 could have performed such a complicated and secret operation.

Water and Air

Imagine being underwater on a submarine for two months. You would need oxygen to breathe and fresh water to drink. Both of these can be taken from the ocean water that surrounds the submarine.

Salt water from the ocean is heated until it becomes vapor, which eliminates the salt. The vapor is then cooled and collected as fresh drinking water. Oxygen generators remove oxygen from seawater, releasing breathable air.

Keeping the air on a sub clean is also important. When people breathe, they exhale a gas called carbon dioxide. Breathing in too much carbon dioxide can be deadly. Because of this, the air on board a sub must be "scrubbed." It passes through filters called scrubbers, which remove the carbon dioxide, leaving only clean oxygen to breathe.

Unmanned Underwater Vehicles (UUVs)

Underwater drones can operate underwater without a human crew. There are two types: those that are remotely operated and those that are autonomous (AUVs)—operating independently of human input, like a robot. The US Navy is using and testing various UUV designs to perform a variety of missions, including reconnaissance, mine detection, and search and salvage. In December 2014, the navy completed tests on the GhostSwimmer UUV, which is approximately 5 feet (1.5 m) long and 100 pounds (45.3 kilograms) and can operate in water depths ranging from 10 inches (25.4 cm) to 300 feet (91.4 m). With its oscillating tail fin, it mimics the shape and swimming style of a large fish.

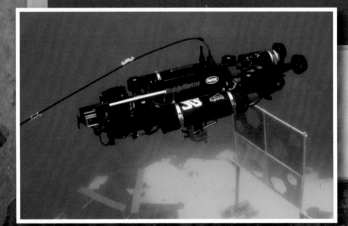

An autonomous underwater vehicle (AUV) navigates through an obstacle course during an underwater test.

Why Are Submarines So Important?

Submarine technology has improved over the years, greatly increasing submarines' capabilities and importance to the United States. But there are three major reasons the US Navy continues to employ them.

The first reason is stealth. This is the ability to move quietly and secretly. The second is agility. This is the ability to travel quickly and easily to places no other vehicle can reach. The third is endurance. This is the ability to remain on patrol, hidden, for long periods of time. Submarines can slip into the most highly guarded regions of the world undetected. They can carry missiles capable of destroying another submarine, a ship, or a target on land.

As submarines are used more often in dangerous war zones, the threat to their crews grows greater. Underwater mines are a constant danger. So are antiship cruise missiles fired from other subs.

Computer and communications systems work together to make submarines safer and better at what they do. Through Internet-like hookups using satellites, submarines can instantly share voice and data information with other subs, ships, and planes. In the future, these systems will operate even faster.

Technicians are working to connect certain systems on board subs so the systems will operate together and make all kinds of information readily available to the crewmen who use them. These systems include sonar, which helps locate targets underwater, and radar, which sends out radio waves to help locate targets in the air and on the ground. Voice communications systems, weapons systems, and computer data information systems will also be part of this network. New sonar equipment will be better at detecting mines and icebergs under the sea in time to safely move away from these dangers.

Whatever other new technology comes along in the future, the mission of America's submarines will stay the same. They will search, observe, and protect. And they will use the darkness beneath the waves to carry out their missions in secrecy.

Sailors aboard the USS *Seawolf* man the main control watch.

Virginia-Class Subs

The newest and best fast attack submarines ever built for the US Navy are the Virginia-class subs. They are the first subs designed for a variety of open-ocean and close-to-shore, or "littoral," missions.

One thing that helps with these missions is a new type of periscope. Instead of a traditional periscope, Virginia-class subs use two photonics masts, which extend up from the hull. Each of these masts contains several high-resolution digital cameras equipped with infrared sensors. Infrared technology allows pictures to be taken even in very low light.

Signals from the photonics masts are sent through fiber-optic cables (like the ones used for phone and Internet connections on land) to computers on board the subs. The signals provide images that can be shared via a computer network with other subs, ships, or people on land.

Developed during the late 1990s and early 2000s, the first Virginia-class sub, the USS *Virginia*, was commissioned, or put into service, in June 2004 and is in operational use today.

The commanding officer of a Virginia-class fast attack submarine demonstrates the photonics mast.

What Happens to an Old Submarine?

When the US Navy decides that an old submarine is no longer worthy of being in the fleet, that sub is decommissioned, or retired. Some decommissioned subs are taken apart, and their metal is recycled. The dangerous nuclear reactors on subs used to be disposed of at sea. Now they are buried in special nuclear waste dumps in Oregon and Washington State.

Other subs are given to the US Maritime Administration. These subs are used in case of a national emergency. They can also be used if more subs are needed during a war. Governments of other countries can pay to use a decommissioned US sub for a certain length of time.

Decommissioned subs might also be used for research purposes, or for navy experiments. They might even be intentionally sunk in the sea and used for target practice! Practice-shooting torpedoes at actual subs helps build skills among submarine crew members.

Still other subs become historic memorials. They are like floating museums. The USS *Nautilus*, the world's first nuclear-powered sub, is one example. It is part of the US Navy Force Museum in Groton, Connecticut. There, visitors can walk through the *Nautilus* and see how crewmen lived and worked at sea. You can visit other decommissioned submarines that have become museums in many cities around the country.

6

So You Want to Become a Submariner?

Men and women who serve on submarines are some of the most highly trained and skilled people in the navy. They must understand a lot about math, physics, chemistry, and engineering. Everyone on board a submarine, no matter what the job is, must know how to operate, maintain, and repair the major systems on board the sub.

They must know how to work the electrical systems, the nuclear reactor, the sonar equipment, and the weapons systems and how to drive the sub. They must also be able to work as cooks and store clerks.

Crew on a sub must also be able to live in a small space, often for months at a time. They must be able to get along with a hundred or so other people living and working very closely together.

Serving on a submarine is voluntary and very competitive. But not everyone who wants to be on a sub gets to serve on one. Sailors who request submarine duty undergo psychological testing to see if they can handle the cramped living quarters. These tests also help to find out if sailors can work closely with the others on board the sub while being submerged.

A working submarine and its crew are the result of the efforts of many specially trained people. The vessel itself is the result of the great skill of submarine designers and technicians. The design of a sub must allow it to move smoothly through deep water. Because of the limited space, the interior design must use every inch of space efficiently. Great engineering skill is also needed to create the sonar, weapons, day-to-day living, and other systems on board.

In addition to the technical, engineering, and scientific skill that goes into the creation and smooth operation of a submarine, human skill is needed as well. Crewmen must operate, maintain, and repair the equipment. The captain must command the vessel, taking into account the needs of the mission, the needs of the crew, and the capability of the submarine. And the crew must work as a team.

Extensive Training

Every crew member on board a sub has undergone months of training. Crew members learn to operate the submarine's systems and equipment in a classroom, and then they practice on board a sub while still in port. In addition, interactive training manuals on computers give an in-depth look at all a crewman needs to know.

Virtual reality trainers are also used in the teaching of submarine crewmen. Wearing virtual reality goggles, students sit at a model of a submarine control room, weapons stations, and communications station. Trainees practice piloting a sub in and out of port. They practice submerging and bringing a sub back to the surface.

The virtual reality system can change the conditions a trainee faces in the scene he is working with. It can alter the weather, ocean

Women on Submarines

Until recently, women were not allowed to serve on submarines. In 2010, the Department of the Navy changed its policy and began to allow qualified women to serve on submarines. The first group of nuclear-trained women officers started serving on ballistic missile submarines—larger than fast attack submarines—in 2011. In January 2015, the first group of women reported aboard the fast attack submarine USS *Minnesota*. Enlisted women are scheduled to first report for duty on submarines in 2016.

Women are now being integrated into US Navy nuclear sub crews.

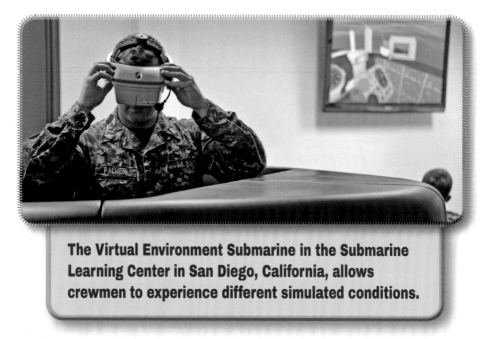

The Virtual Environment Submarine in the Submarine Learning Center in San Diego, California, allows crewmen to experience different simulated conditions.

conditions, and the presence of other vessels. It can also create crisis situations, such as accidents on board or attacks by opposing subs or ships. This teaches the trainee how to react to different situations.

Final training comes during test runs at sea. There, combat situations are simulated. Torpedoes without explosives are fired, sonar is monitored to detect the presence of opposing vessels, and stealth surveillance is practiced.

Careers After the Military

When they get out of the navy, many crewmen who served on subs work in technical jobs, such as repairing engines on cars, boats, or planes. They also can work in the communications field, operating technical broadcasting equipment. Many submarine sailors and officers use their knowledge of nuclear systems to find jobs working at nuclear power plants. Their training and experience as part of a special group living and working under the sea, operating sophisticated, specialized equipment, helps them do many kinds of jobs.

TIMELINE

1775—The first military submarine, the *Turtle*, is built.

1862—First US Navy submarine, the *Alligator*, is launched with hand-operated propellers for use in the Civil War.

1900—The first "modern" submarine, USS *Holland*, is built, using a gasoline-powered engine on the ocean's surface and a battery for traveling underwater.

1904—The first diesel-powered submarine, the French *Aigrette*, is built.

1955—The first nuclear-powered submarine, USS *Nautilus* (SSN-571), becomes operational.

1959—First US Navy ballistic missile submarine, USS *George Washington* (SSBN-598), is commissioned.

2010—The US Navy reverses its ban on women on submarines.

A crew member of the USS *George Washington* works at a defense center for joint military exercises.

GLOSSARY

ballast tanks—Tanks on a submarine that fill with air to keep the sub afloat and fill with water to help it submerge.

berthing area—The place where submarine crewmen sleep.

bunker—A reinforced room made of steel and concrete, sometimes underground, used for protection during a battle.

commission—To put into service or to be given a particular function.

cruise missile—Weapon that flies through the air to strike a target on land.

decommission—To put out of service.

decompression—Changes in pressure.

helmsman—The crew member on a submarine who adjusts the rudder, or the flap that steers the sub left or right.

hull—The outer covering of a ship or submarine.

intelligence—Information about a country's military plans and weapons.

littoral—The part of the ocean that is closest to shore, up to 600 feet (183 m) away from the shoreline.

periscope—A device on a submarine that sticks out of the water and allows the crew to see what is happening on the surface, while the sub is still underwater.

planesman—The crew member on a submarine that adjusts the diving planes, the flaps that steer the sub up or down.

radar—Radio waves sent out to locate objects on the ground or in the air.

reconnaissance—Military observation of a region in order to locate an enemy or to ascertain strategic features.

sonar—Equipment on a submarine that sends out sound waves to locate objects underwater or to listen to the sounds made by other submarines or ships.

submerge—To go underwater.

surface—To rise up to the top of a body of water.

surveillance—Watching in secret, spying.

torpedo—Weapon carried by submarines, meant to move underwater and strike another sub or a ship.

vertical launch tube—Metal tube aimed to fire a weapon into the air.

FURTHER READING

BOOKS

LaVO, Carl. *The Galloping Ghost: The Extraordinary Life of Submarine Legend Eugene Fluckey.* Annapolis, Md.: Naval Institute Press, 2011.

Scott, James. *The War Below: The Story of Three Submarines That Battled Japan.* New York: Simon & Schuster, 2014.

Spilling, Michael. *Weapons of War Submarines 1940–Present.* New York: Chartwell Books, 2013.

Walker, Sally M. *Secrets of a Civil War Submarine: Solving the Mysteries of the H. L. Hunley.* Minneapolis, Minn.: Carolrhoda, 2005.

WEB SITES

hnsa.org/hnsa-ships
A full list of submarine museums around the world

navy.com/careers/nuclear-power.html
How to pursue a career in submarines

science.howstuffworks.com/submarine.htm
Details on how a submarine works

USS *Ohio* nuclear-powered submarine

INDEX